SOUTHWEST WISCONSIN LIBRARY SYSTEM

S0-BIJ-012

WITHDRAWN

Dodgeville Public Library
139 S Iowa Street
Dodgeville WI 53533

INSIDE THE
NFL

CHICAGO
BEARS

BY ROBERT COOPER

SportsZone

An Imprint of Abdo Publishing
abdobooks.com

abdobooks.com

Published by Abdo Publishing, a division of ABDO, PO Box 398166, Minneapolis, Minnesota 55439. Copyright © 2020 by Abdo Consulting Group, Inc. International copyrights reserved in all countries. No part of this book may be reproduced in any form without written permission from the publisher. SportsZone™ is a trademark and logo of Abdo Publishing.

Printed in the United States of America, North Mankato, Minnesota
022019
092019

THIS BOOK CONTAINS
RECYCLED MATERIALS

Cover Photo: Greg Trott/AP Images
Interior Photos: Red McLendon/AP Images, 5; Bill Smith/Getty Images Sport/Getty Images, 6; Phil Sandlin/AP Images, 11, 43; AP Images, 13, 15, 17, 19, 21, 23, 25, 30; NFL Photos/AP Images, 27; David Stluka/AP Images, 33; Rick Osentoski/AP Images, 37; Al Messerschmidt/AP Images, 39; Greg Trott/AP Images, 40

Editor: Patrick Donnelly
Series Designer: Craig Hinton

Library of Congress Control Number: 2018965091

Publisher's Cataloging-in-Publication Data

Names: Cooper, Robert, author.
Title: Chicago Bears / by Robert Cooper.
Description: Minneapolis, Minnesota : Abdo Publishing, 2020 | Series: Inside the NFL | Includes online resources and index.
Identifiers: ISBN 9781532118418 (lib. bdg.) | ISBN 9781532172595 (ebook) | ISBN 9781644941034 (pbk.)
Subjects: LCSH: Chicago Bears (Football team)--Juvenile literature. | National Football League--Juvenile literature. | Football teams--Juvenile literature. | American football--Juvenile literature.
Classification: DDC 796.33264--dc23

TABLE OF
CONTENTS

CHAPTER 1
"SWEETNESS" AND THE SUPER BOWL 4

CHAPTER 2
NEW TEAM, NEW LEAGUE 12

CHAPTER 3
73–0 AND THE GLORY YEARS 18

CHAPTER 4
A TOUGH TEAM 24

CHAPTER 5
GETTING BACK TO THE SUPER BOWL 32

CHAPTER 6
HOPE FOR THE NEXT GREAT QB 36

TIMELINE   42
QUICK STATS   44
QUOTES AND ANECDOTES   45
GLOSSARY   46
MORE INFORMATION   47
ONLINE RESOURCES   47
INDEX   48
ABOUT THE AUTHOR   48

"SWEETNESS" AND THE SUPER BOWL

He was quick and difficult to tackle. But he also could hit defensive players with force. His nickname, "Sweetness," described his pleasing-to-watch play on the field. It also was an appropriate word for him off the field, as he played jokes on his teammates and enjoyed life.

He was Walter Payton, perhaps the greatest player in Bears history.

Payton was not well known at the beginning of his National Football League (NFL) career. He had played at Jackson State, a historically black university in Mississippi. Because of its size, Jackson State did not compete against

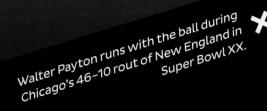
Walter Payton runs with the ball during Chicago's 46–10 rout of New England in Super Bowl XX.

Payton gains some of his 275 rushing yards in the Bears' 10–7 win over the Vikings in November 1977.

the largest schools in the country. But the game films could not lie. Payton was a sure thing. So in the 1975 NFL Draft, new Bears general manager Jim Finks selected him in the first round, fourth overall. Payton was the first key acquisition in a long process that built the Bears into Super Bowl champions.

Payton had an average rookie season. But he emerged as a top NFL running back in 1976 with 1,390 rushing yards. In 1977 Payton led the Bears to their first playoff appearance since 1963. He gained 1,852 yards and averaged 5.5 yards per carry. Included was a November 20 game at Chicago's Soldier Field in which Payton ran for 275 yards, then an NFL record. This helped the Bears edge the Minnesota Vikings 10–7.

"You Chicago people are spoiled by Payton—he's a phenomenon," longtime Vikings coach Bud Grant said.

Payton gained thousands of yards while the Bears' overall performance was average at best. They made the playoffs with a 9–5 record in 1977. But the Bears slumped in 1978. They went back to the postseason as a wild card with a 10–6 mark in 1979.

MORE ON "SWEETNESS"

In addition to his rushing and receiving skills, Walter Payton was a surprisingly good passer on trick plays. He completed 11 passes during his career, eight of them for touchdowns, including one to quarterback Jim McMahon in a game in 1985.

Payton was also famous for repeatedly running up a steep hill in Arlington Heights, Illinois, in the offseason to improve his conditioning. When asked in 1983 about the secret of his success, Payton replied, "Not staying in one place for very long."

After he retired, Payton served as a volunteer assistant basketball coach at a high school in Schaumburg, Illinois, among other activities. His son, Jarrett Payton, played running back briefly in the NFL for the Tennessee Titans in 2005.

They then had four mediocre years in a row. But the team steadily gathered talent, largely through the draft.

Defensive end Dan Hampton arrived in 1979. Linebacker Mike Singletary came aboard in 1981. They drafted quarterback Jim McMahon in 1982. Defensive end Richard Dent, defensive back Dave Duerson, tackle Jimbo Covert, and wide receiver Willie Gault were part of a strong draft class in 1983. That draft was Finks's last as Chicago's general manager. Seven players who would start on the 1985 Super Bowl XX team came from the 1983 draft.

The most important move off the field was owner George Halas's hiring of Mike Ditka as head coach in early 1982. Halas was impressed by a letter Ditka wrote in which he expressed a desire to coach the team for which he had played in the 1960s. By 1984 the Bears had put together a winning squad. But it was too late for Halas to enjoy. "Papa Bear" died at 88 on October 31, 1983. In tribute, the Bears took the field in 1984 wearing the initials GSH on their sleeves. The Bears have worn the tribute ever since.

The defense, built by defensive coordinator Buddy Ryan, allowed just 248 points in 16 games in 1984. That year the Bears won their first division title since 1963. They played even better in 1985. They gave up only 198 points in 16 games. The Bears became a national sensation by starting out 12–0. Included in this stretch were back-to-back shutouts of the Dallas Cowboys (44–0) and the Atlanta Falcons (36–0).

Everyone paid attention to 335-pound William "Refrigerator" Perry, the team's top draft choice in 1985. Despite his size, "The Fridge" was athletic enough to dunk a basketball. And in a *Monday Night Football* game on October 21, Perry took center stage. Ditka decided to settle some old grudges from his playing days against Green Bay Packers coach Forrest Gregg. He used Perry, a defensive tackle, at fullback to score a rushing touchdown in the Bears' 23–7 home win over the Packers. Two weeks later, Ditka had Perry line up on offense again, this time in Green Bay. He caught a 4-yard touchdown pass from McMahon.

WHY THE "46" DEFENSE?

The Bears' remarkable defense in the 1985 season was called the "46" defense. It was named after the uniform number of tough-guy safety Doug Plank, who actually had not played for the team since 1982. Buddy Ryan became Chicago's defensive coordinator in 1978. He created the 46 defense in 1981. The defense featured a unique front, designed to confuse the quarterback. The defensive line was shifted dramatically to the weak side—the opposite end from the offense's tight end. This front made it considerably harder for offensive lines to execute blocking assignments.

Star quarterback Dan Marino and the Miami Dolphins spoiled Chicago's bid for a perfect 1985 season with a 38–24 victory on Monday Night Football. The loss did not stop some of the Bears, led by Payton and Singletary, from taping the famed "Super Bowl Shuffle" rap video the next day. Such was the confidence of the team.

They bounced back to win their final three regular-season games to finish 15–1. But the best was yet to come. In the postseason, the Bears blanked the New York Giants 21–0 and the Los Angeles Rams 24–0 in frigid conditions at Soldier Field. Then it was on to the Super Bowl in New Orleans, where they would face the New England Patriots.

It seemed that the whole world was watching the colorful Bears. They did not disappoint. They routed the Patriots 46–10 in front of 73,818 fans in the Superdome on January 26, 1986. The Bears scored in the air and on the ground, including on a 1-yard run by Perry. The only disappointment for Bears fans was that Payton did not score in the blowout.

It was a season that could hardly be repeated—and it was not. The defense was actually even stingier the next year, allowing just 187 points in a 14–2 season. But the Bears had quarterback problems. McMahon battled injuries. From the

From *left*, Willie Gault, Steve McMichael, coach Mike Ditka, William Perry, and Maury Buford are Super Bowl XX champions.

1986 season through 1991, the Bears won just two of their seven playoff games. They would never return to the Super Bowl under Ditka. He was fired after a 5–11 season in 1992. But Chicago would never forget 1985.

One by one, the 1985 Bears retired or moved on to other teams. No one was missed more, of course, than Payton. He retired after his thirteenth season in 1987 with an NFL-record 16,726 rushing yards. His 125 total touchdowns were the second most in league history at that point.

Payton might have been the most beloved player in the history of a franchise that traces its roots back to the beginning of the NFL.

CHAPTER 2

NEW TEAM, NEW LEAGUE

The Chicago Bears—one of the country's most popular professional sports teams—and the NFL itself began in an unlikely way. Both were founded by a man who had played right field for the New York Yankees before Babe Ruth.

All of this happened in 1920. George Halas was a native of Chicago's West Side and a University of Illinois graduate. He had spent two months of the 1919 season as a Yankees outfielder. He played a few games in right field and hit just .091. Ruth arrived the next season. The rest was history. Obviously not cut out for baseball, Halas looked for work.

Industrialist A. E. Staley was eager to field a competitive football team to represent his cornstarch company in Decatur, Illinois. He contacted Halas after getting a

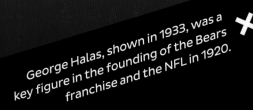

George Halas, shown in 1933, was a key figure in the founding of the Bears franchise and the NFL in 1920.

recommendation from University of Illinois football star Ed "Dutch" Sternaman. Halas worked as a Staley employee and a player-coach of the new team. Halas and Sternaman recruited top college talent from all over the Midwest. At the same time, Canton (Ohio) Bulldogs owner Ralph Hay wanted to organize a professional football league. Halas figured his new team, the Decatur Staleys, ought to join. The organizers met at Hay's Hupmobile car dealership in Canton on September 17, 1920.

The men formed the American Professional Football Association (APFA). Joining the Staleys were the Bulldogs, Akron Pros, Buffalo All-Americans, Chicago Cardinals, Chicago Tigers, Cleveland Tigers, Columbus Panhandles, Dayton Triangles, Detroit Heralds, Hammond Pros, Muncie Flyers, Rochester Jeffersons, and Rock Island Independents. Former Olympics star Jim Thorpe was named league president.

The Decatur Staleys finished their first season, in 1920, with a 5–1–2 record in league play and a 10–1–2 mark overall. The Staleys tied Akron 0–0 in a playoff game at Wrigley Field in Chicago.

In 1921 Staley decided to not support the effort any longer. However, he gave Halas and Sternaman $5,000 in "seed money" to move the team to the big city. They struck a deal for the use

Shown in 1930, Red Grange, *left*, and Bronko Nagurski formed a strong combination in the Bears' backfield.

of Cubs Park—which would be renamed Wrigley Field in 1927—for 15 percent of ticket profits. Then, in 1922, Halas and Sternaman dropped the name Staleys in favor of the Bears. The Chicago Cubs baseball team was already playing in the same stadium. Halas figured football players are bigger than baseball players. Since bears are larger versions of cubs, Halas decided to call his football team the Bears. In 1922 the APFA also chose a new name: the National Football League.

The Bears and the NFL struggled for attention and fans until November 22, 1925. On that date, Halas and Sternaman signed running back Red Grange to a contract. Grange was

STAYING INDOORS

Arena football was still 54 years away when bad weather forced the Bears and Portsmouth Spartans to play the first indoor title game in 1932. The improvised field in Chicago Stadium was sized like arena ball: only 80 yards long. Hash marks were first used in this game and straw was put over the surface, which had just hosted a circus. The Bears won 9–0.

a University of Illinois player considered the greatest in college football. "The Galloping Ghost" and the Bears were booked on a barnstorming tour with four games in eight days in Philadelphia, Boston, New York, and Detroit. Huge crowds, including 70,000 at New York's Polo Grounds, turned out. Grange and agent C. C. Pyle split $250,000. The Bears earned $100,000. Both were huge amounts at the time. Soon, bruising fullback Bronko Nagurski joined Grange in the backfield. Halas continued to play for the Bears in addition to coaching them. He played end on offense and defense.

The money from the Grange tour did not last long. The Bears lost $18,000 in 1932, during the heart of the Great Depression. That year, they played the first pro football playoff game indoors—at the old Chicago Stadium.

Halas had stopped playing after the 1928 season. But he was still the team's coach and part owner. He wanted to buy out Sternaman to be the Bears' only owner. He barely made a

✕ The Giants' Dale Burnett closes in on Bears ball carrier Beattie Feathers, *far left*, in October 1937 at the Polo Grounds in New York.

deadline on August 9, 1933, to give Sternaman $38,000 for his share of the club. The Bears went on to win the NFL title that year with a 23–21 victory over the visiting New York Giants. Chicago lost the NFL Championship Game in 1934 (to the host Giants) and again in 1937 (to visiting Washington).

The best was yet to come. The Bears drafted a quarterback named Sid Luckman out of Columbia University in 1939. Luckman's arrival led to the most successful era in team history.

CHAPTER 3

73-0 AND THE GLORY YEARS

When George Halas signed Sid Luckman in 1939, he knew he had the man to help him change pro football.

The NFL game was centered on running the ball in a "single-wing" formation. Most teams did not pass much. But Halas devised a "T-formation." In this formation, a quarterback lined up with two running backs behind him and had the option of passing or running. The smart Luckman was just the man to head up the "T-formation." It later was celebrated in the team fight song, "Bear Down, Chicago Bears."

"There was all the spinning for handoffs or fakes, and new signal-calling," Luckman remembered of learning the complicated new system. "All the fundamentals were

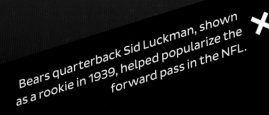

Bears quarterback Sid Luckman, shown as a rookie in 1939, helped popularize the forward pass in the NFL.

JUST ONE CHANCE

The only real chance that Washington had in its 73–0 loss to the Bears in the 1940 NFL Championship Game came with the Bears leading 7–0 in the first quarter. Charley Malone could not reel in a potential touchdown pass from Sammy Baugh as the Chicago defense held firm. It was all Bears from there. Baugh was asked afterward whether the outcome would have been different had Malone hung on to the ball. "Yes," he quipped. "The score would have been 73–6."

different from what I had played as a tailback."

Luckman played part time in 1939. He then became the starter in 1940. The Bears excelled as a result. Backs Bill Osmanski, George McAfee, and Ray Nolting, and linemen Bulldog Turner, Joe Stydahar, Danny Fortmann, and George Musso helped Luckman. Chicago headed for a showdown with equally powerful Washington and quarterback "Slingin'" Sammy Baugh in the championship game. After his team beat the Bears 7–3 earlier in the season, Washington owner George Preston Marshall said the Bears were "quitters . . . just a bunch of crybabies. They fold up when the going gets tough."

Inspired by the insult, the Bears took out their frustrations on Washington with Marshall watching helplessly at old Griffith Stadium in Washington. Osmanski ran 68 yards for a touchdown early. The Bears scored so often, Luckman's strong right arm was hardly needed. The Bears ran wild in the

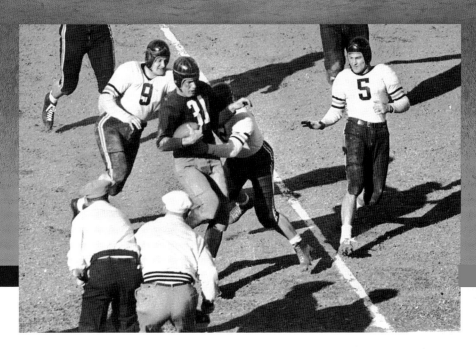

Luckman, who also played defense, tackles Washington's Jimmy Johnston in the Bears' 73–0 rout in the 1940 NFL title game.

most lopsided championship game ever—a 73–0 blowout. Chicago defenders helped the cause by running back three interceptions for touchdowns.

The legendary victory helped cement the Bears' status as "the Monsters of the Midway." They were on course to win three more championships in the next five years with Luckman at the controls. The team was even more dominating in 1941 with a 10–1 regular season. Chicago tied the archrival Green Bay Packers for the Western Division title. The Bears dominated the Packers 33–14 in a divisional playoff game before more than 43,000 at Wrigley Field. A week later, just 13,341 showed up to watch the Bears thump the Giants 37–9 in the NFL title game.

With the country entering World War II at the end of 1941, Halas left to serve in the US Navy during the 1943 season. But Luckman stayed on to lead the Bears to an 8–1–1 record. The title-clinching game had been spurred by Bronko Nagurski, who came out of a six-year retirement to help fill in for players away in the military. "The Bronk" rushed for 84 fourth-quarter yards on 16 carries. The Bears rallied for a 35–24 win over the crosstown Cardinals in the regular-season finale. Then Luckman put on a show against Baugh and Washington in the title game at Wrigley Field. The Bears' quarterback threw five touchdown passes in a 41–21 triumph.

The Bears slipped a bit in 1944 and 1945. By this time, Luckman was serving in the US Navy but still stationed in the United States. He could not practice with the team during the week. But he could play in Chicago's games on the weekends. By 1946 the war was over and he returned to the team full time. That year the Bears were as strong as ever. They finished 8–2–1. Halas was back as coach as well. This time they faced the Giants for the title. Going back to his old tailback days, Luckman was able to use his legs to surprise effect. He employed a rarely used trick play called "Bingo-Keep-It."

Halas and Luckman compare notes the day before the Bears' 24–14 win over the Giants in the 1946 NFL title game.

"When I got the snap, I faked to [George] McAfee and he headed around left end with the Giants in wild pursuit," Luckman said. "I just tucked the ball against my leg and danced around right end. I got two great blocks from [Bulldog] Turner and [Ray] Bray and went the 19 yards for a touchdown." The visiting Bears won 24–14.

The Bears continued to contend for the Western Division title before the end of Luckman's career in 1950. But they did not get back to an NFL title game. Their greatest era had ended. But the Bears' place among pro football's legends was secure.

CHAPTER 4

A TOUGH TEAM

In the seasons after Sid Luckman retired, the Bears were not known for their quarterbacks. Rather, they established an identity as a bruising squad that would leave you battered no matter the final score. Sometimes, that was the Bears' biggest accomplishment. They had three losing seasons in the 1950s.

George Halas made mistakes in judging quarterbacks. He acquired former University of Texas star Bobby Layne in a trade shortly after the Pittsburgh Steelers selected Layne with the third pick of the 1948 draft. But one year later, Halas cut Layne in favor of former Notre Dame star Johnny Lujack, their No. 1 pick in 1946. Layne went on to lead the Detroit Lions to NFL titles in 1952 and 1953. George Blanda was a Bears backup through much of the 1950s. He was released and then became a star with the Houston Oilers in the new

Linebacker Bill George, shown in 1963, was a Bears standout from 1952 to 1965.

BREAKING BARRIERS

In 1952 halfback Eddie Macon from the College of the Pacific became the Bears' first black player. The next season, the Bears also fielded the first black quarterback in NFL history. Former Michigan State University standout Willie Thrower played in one game and went 3-for-8 for 27 yards.

American Football League in 1960. Ed Brown, an unremarkable player, was the Bears' starting quarterback throughout the second half of the 1950s. He threw to skilled ends Harlon Hill and Jim Dooley.

The best-known, and perhaps toughest, Bear of the decade was middle linebacker Bill George. He started playing for the team in 1952. George invented the position of middle linebacker by playing off the line. He backed up end Ed Sprinkle, dubbed "The Meanest Man in Football" by *Colliers* magazine.

"A lot said I played dirty," Sprinkle said. "That's just not true. Mean maybe, but not dirty. . . . A guy wouldn't have lasted very long in the league if he played dirty regularly."

George was the defense's star. Fullback Rick Casares provided toughness on offense. In 1956 Halas turned over the head coach's job to Paddy Driscoll. That year the team finally reached the NFL title game again. However, the New York Giants wiped them out, 47–7. Halas took the reins back in 1958.

Bears running back Ronnie Bull takes off on a run against the Giants during the Bears' 14–10 win in the 1963 NFL Championship Game at Wrigley Field.

The Bears finished 8–4 in four other seasons in the 1950s. But they always fell short of the playoffs.

The Bears fell further back when the Green Bay Packers became an NFL dynasty under coach Vince Lombardi in the early 1960s. A 49–0 Packers thrashing of the Bears in 1962 greatly upset Halas, who aggressively prepared his team in 1963 to stop Green Bay's star-studded attack. The Chicago defense was led by George and fellow linebackers

Joe Fortunato and Larry Morris, linemen Doug Atkins and Stan Jones, and defensive backs Rosey Taylor and Dave Whitsell. All rose to the occasion like never before. The defense allowed just 144 points in 14 games.

Meanwhile, tight end Mike Ditka and wide receiver Johnny Morris chipped in with clutch catches. The Bears won the Western Division with an 11–1–2 record. They again met the Giants in the title game. This time the contest was at a frozen Wrigley Field on December 29, 1963. The temperature was just nine degrees. Again, the defense held firm in a 14–10 victory. The Bears battered veteran Giants quarterback Y. A. Tittle. Thousands of fans who could not get into Wrigley Field watched on closed-circuit TV at theaters around the Chicago area. The game telecast was blacked out on local TV.

The title would be Halas's last as Bears coach. Chicago was hurt by injuries and by the tragic deaths of running back Willie Galimore and wide receiver John "Bo" Farrington in an offseason automobile accident. The Bears went just 5–9 in 1964.

They had a brief revival after they acquired two future Hall of Famers back to back in the first round of the 1965 NFL Draft. Linebacker Dick Butkus was a Chicago native who played at the

University of Illinois. Running back Gale Sayers played his college ball at the University of Kansas.

Butkus, taken third overall in the first round, was an immediate star on defense in 1965. Sayers, selected with the next pick, stunned the NFL with a record 22 touchdowns in 14 games as a rookie. His greatest game was on December 12, 1965. That day he scored six touchdowns in a 61–20 win over the San Francisco 49ers at Wrigley Field. Four were rushing touchdowns, another came on an 80-yard pass, and the final touchdown was an electrifying 85-yard punt return. Sayers might have scored a seventh touchdown that day, but Halas pulled him from the game because it was a blowout.

Sayers was such an elusive runner that defenders often thought they had stopped him before finding out he had slipped away.

"It was on an 80-yard run on a screen pass he made against us," Los Angeles Rams defensive tackle Rosey Grier recalled.

MADE INTO A MOVIE

The friendship between Gale Sayers and fellow Bears running back Brian Piccolo, who died of cancer at age 26 in 1970, was made into the famed 1971 TV movie *Brian's Song*. Billy Dee Williams and James Caan starred. Jack Warden played George Halas.

The Bears were mediocre in the late 1960s. But running back Gale Sayers provided plenty of thrills for the team's fans.

"I hit him so hard near the line of scrimmage, I thought my shoulder must have busted him in two. I heard a roar from the crowd and figured he had fumbled. Then there he was, 15 yards downfield and heading for the end zone."

Despite having Sayers and Butkus, the Bears were average at best. Halas finally retired as coach in early 1968. He turned the team over to longtime assistant coach Jim Dooley. But the Bears collapsed in 1969. They finished 1–13, the worst record in team history.

Between 1969 and 1975, Chicago had a 28–69–1 record. Sayers's and Butkus's Hall of Fame careers ended early because

DICK BUTKUS

Dick Butkus was the most authentic Chicago Bear. He grew up on the far southeast side of the city and attended Chicago Vocational High School. He played fullback in addition to linebacker in high school. Staying close to home, Butkus then starred for the University of Illinois.

Those good hands on offense led him to play on special teams in the NFL. Butkus actually caught two point-after-touchdown passes when the attempted kicks failed.

He turned his terror-on-the-field reputation into money after his pro football career. Nicknamed "Super Crunch" for his violent style at middle linebacker, Butkus moved to Hollywood and became an actor after his last Bears game in 1973.

Butkus and Gale Sayers were both drafted by the Bears in 1965, one pick apart. Their numbers (Butkus 51 and Sayers 40) were retired together during a game in 1994.

of knee injuries. Mediocre quarterback play prevailed. The only real change in the team was leaving Wrigley Field after 50 seasons for the rundown Soldier Field stadium near Lake Michigan in 1971.

Finally, the Halas family had enough of losing. As the 1974 season started, George Halas Jr., then the team president, hired dynamic former Minnesota Vikings general manager Jim Finks to become the Bears' general manager. Finks's first No. 1 draft pick, Walter Payton in 1975, started the team's long march toward its 1985 Super Bowl season. However, getting back to the big game after that would prove to be a major challenge.

CHAPTER 5

GETTING BACK TO THE SUPER BOWL

With Walter Payton on board, the Bears began to build a team that would contend for a championship. Once that dream was realized by dominating the New England Patriots in Super Bowl XX, fans expected them to stay on top for years to come. After all, they still had a core of Payton, coach Mike Ditka, and a suffocating defense.

Chicago won 11 or more regular-season games in five of the six years after the Super Bowl season. But the Bears could not get back to the big game. They began rebuilding after Ditka was fired as coach and made just one playoff appearance the rest of the 1990s.

Devin Hester helped the Bears with his dynamic special teams play.

PEANUT

Cornerback Charles "Peanut" Tillman was a star in the Bears secondary from 2003 to 2014. He had 36 interceptions and returned eight for touchdowns, the most in Bears history. He could also cause fumbles and was known for the "Peanut Punch." When he had the chance, Tillman swung his fist directly at the ball, knocking it out of the ball carrier's grasp.

This period of Bears history was defined by a search for a quarterback. They tried 13 different starting quarterbacks in the 1990s. This entire era of decline was made even worse by the sad news of Payton's death at age 45 from a rare liver disease on November 1, 1999.

With new coach Lovie Smith in 2004, the Bears also built a quality defense. It was led by middle linebacker Brian Urlacher. He was the team's top draft pick in 2000.

Lance Briggs joined Urlacher at linebacker. Safety Mike Brown anchored the secondary. The Bears jumped to 11–5 and a division title in 2005. But they lost 29–21 to the visiting Carolina Panthers in the divisional playoffs.

The Bears then took the next step, aiming for their return to the Super Bowl in 2006 with a 13–3 season. Chicago was boosted by a great first half of the season from quarterback Rex Grossman. He was a controversial figure who had either been injured or inconsistent since the Bears drafted him in the first round in 2003. Grossman threw for 23 touchdowns but also threw 20 interceptions. Running back Thomas Jones enjoyed a strong season with 1,210 rushing yards. The defense led the league in takeaways as the Bears rolled to Super Bowl XLI against the Indianapolis Colts.

The sensational Devin Hester put the Bears ahead 7–0 in the first quarter with a 92-yard kickoff return. Chicago took a 14–6 lead soon afterward. But the Peyton Manning–led Colts scored 16 straight points. The Bears were still in the game. They trailed 22–17 in the fourth quarter. But then Colts cornerback Kelvin Hayden intercepted a pass by Grossman and ran it back 56 yards for a clinching touchdown. Grossman committed four turnovers in all as the Bears lost 29–17.

Chicago did not get back to the big game after three more mediocre years. Grossman left as a free agent in 2009, and the Bears made a trade to find their next signal caller.

Chicago sent quarterback Kyle Orton and three draft picks, including two in the first round, to the Denver Broncos to acquire promising young quarterback Jay Cutler. Bears fans hoped he would be the third great Bears quarterback after Sid Luckman and Jim McMahon.

CHAPTER 6

HOPE FOR THE NEXT GREAT QB

Jay Cutler got off to a rough start in Chicago. The Bears actually won two fewer games in 2009 with him at the helm. He threw a career-high 26 interceptions, the most in the NFL.

Cutler rebounded slightly in 2010. But much like in 2006, it was the defense that turned the team around. The Bears had signed defensive end Julius Peppers before the season. He tied for the team lead in sacks and made the Pro Bowl. Along with linebackers Brian Urlacher and Lance Briggs, the defense was nearly impossible to run on.

The Bears won their division and made it all the way to the National Football Conference (NFC) Championship Game. They hosted their archrivals, the Green Bay Packers, at Soldier Field. Cutler had played great in the divisional round,

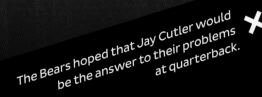

The Bears hoped that Jay Cutler would be the answer to their problems at quarterback.

LINEBACKER TRADITION CONTINUES

Brian Urlacher was inducted into the Pro Football Hall of Fame in his first year of eligibility in 2018. This continued a Bears middle linebacker tradition. Bill George, the first player to star in the middle linebacker position, was inducted in 1974. Dick Butkus followed in 1979, followed by Mike Singletary in 1998.

Chicago has prided itself on strong linebackers. The Bears were fortunate enough to keep the duo of Urlacher and Lance Briggs together for 10 seasons. They combined for 15 Pro Bowl appearances, 38 interceptions, and 56.5 sacks.

In 2018 the Bears drafted someone they hoped would carry on the tradition. They took Roquan Smith from Georgia eighth overall. Smith won the 2017 Butkus Award—named after the Bears legend—as the best college linebacker.

with a pair of touchdown passes and two touchdown runs in a win over the Seattle Seahawks. But he was injured early in the NFC Championship Game, and the Bears had to turn to their backup. Caleb Hanie threw one touchdown pass but also was intercepted twice as the Bears fell to the Packers 21–14.

The Bears have never been successful without a great running back, and with these teams, Matt Forte filled that role. The second-round draft pick in 2008 could run and catch the ball. In each of his eight seasons in Chicago, he accounted for more than 1,200 total yards from scrimmage.

× Brian Urlacher was one of the many outstanding linebackers to play for the Bears.

Cutler's injury problems lingered into 2011. The Bears were 7–3 in games he started but just 1–5 with backups under center. They posted a 10–6 record in 2012, but consecutive losses to Minnesota and Green Bay in December ended their playoff hopes.

The Bears scored the second-most points in the NFL in 2013. But uncharacteristically for Chicago, its defense was one of the worst in the league. Urlacher retired in 2012, and Briggs followed suit in 2014. That was a recipe for disaster that kept the Bears at the bottom of the league.

✕ Mitch Trubisky celebrates one of his six touchdown passes in a victory over the Tampa Bay Buccaneers in 2018.

Though Cutler set almost every Bears career passing record, his inconsistent play didn't help the team get back to the playoffs. He was released after an injury-plagued 2016 season in which the Bears won just three games.

With that bad record came a good draft pick. Bears general manager Ryan Pace scouted a number of high-profile college quarterbacks, hoping one of them could help turn the team around. He ended up choosing Mitch Trubisky from North Carolina with the second pick of the 2017 draft.

The Bears already had signed a starting quarterback in free agent Mike Glennon. But by Week 5, Trubisky got his chance to start. He played in 12 games, throwing seven touchdown passes and seven interceptions. To help him in 2018, the Bears signed free agent wide receiver Allen Robinson and traded for pass-rushing specialist Khalil Mack from the Raiders. Add in a top-10 defense from 2017, and the Bears had reasons for hope.

The 2018 Bears rode that defense and an improving Trubisky to run away with the NFC North title. However, in their first playoff game, the Bears missed a field goal in the final seconds and were upset by the Eagles 16–15.

The 1985 Super Bowl team will always loom large in the memories of Bears fans. That's because no team has managed to surpass their success. Bears fans are always hopeful for the next generation of memorable Monsters of the Midway to come around.

FIGHT SONG

The famed fight song "Bear Down, Chicago Bears," written by Al Hoffman, made its debut in 1941. It remains one of the most stirring team songs in any sport. "Bear Down, Chicago Bears" is part of a list of memorable Chicago team songs that include "Go, Cubs, Go" for the North Side baseball team, "Let's Go-Go-Go, White Sox" for the South Side baseball squad, and "Here Come the Hawks" for the National Hockey League team.

TIMELINE

1920
Bears founder George Halas helps form the American Professional Football Association, which later becomes the NFL, at a Canton, Ohio, auto dealership.

1922
After playing as the Staleys their first two seasons, the team is renamed the Bears.

1925
Running back Red Grange makes his Bears debut before 39,000 fans in Chicago on November 26.

1933
The Bears beat the visiting New York Giants 23–21 on December 17 in the first NFL Championship Game.

1940
Ten Bears score touchdowns as the Monsters of the Midway crush Washington 73–0 on December 8 in the NFL title game at Griffith Stadium.

1941
The Bears beat the Giants 37–9 to win the NFL championship on December 21 at Wrigley Field.

1943
Sid Luckman throws five touchdown passes as the Bears defeat Washington 41–21 on December 26 for the NFL championship at Wrigley Field.

1946
The Bears beat the Giants 24–14 before a then-record NFL title game crowd of 58,346 on December 15 at New York's Polo Grounds.

1963
The Bears intercept five passes by Y. A. Tittle and edge the Giants 14–10 for the NFL crown on December 29 at Wrigley Field.

1965
Gale Sayers scores six touchdowns in a 61–20 win over the San Francisco 49ers on December 12 at Wrigley Field.

1968
Halas retires on May 27 as the winningest coach in football history at the time with 324 victories.

1977
Walter Payton gains a record 275 rushing yards in Chicago's 10–7 win over the Minnesota Vikings on November 20 at Soldier Field.

1982
Mike Ditka, a former Bears tight end, is hired as the team's coach on January 20.

1983
Halas dies at 88 on October 31.

1986
The Bears thrash the New England Patriots 46–10 to win Super Bowl XX on January 26 in New Orleans.

Behind three first-team All-Pro players the Bears defense allows the fewest points in the NFL, leading Chicago to its first division title in eight years.

1987
Payton plays the final regular-season game in his career as Chicago defeats the Raiders 6–3 in Los Angeles on December 27. Payton rushes 20 times for 82 yards.

2007
Chicago scores first in Super Bowl XLI against Indianapolis via Devin Hester's kickoff return. But the Bears lose 29–17 to the Colts on February 4 in Miami.

2011
With new quarterback Jay Cutler, the Bears host the NFC Championship Game but fall to the Green Bay Packers 21–14 on January 23.

2017
The Bears draft quarterback Mitchell Trubisky in the first round, the highest they have selected a quarterback since taking Bob Williams in 1951.

2018

QUICK STATS

FRANCHISE HISTORY

Decatur Staleys (1920)
Chicago Staleys (1921)
Chicago Bears (1922–)

SUPER BOWLS
(wins in bold)

1985 (XX), 2006 (XLI)

NFL CHAMPIONSHIP GAMES *(wins in bold)*

1933, 1934, 1937, **1940**, **1941**, 1942, **1943**, **1946**, 1956, **1963**

NFC CHAMPIONSHIP GAMES *(since 1970 AFL-NFL merger)*

1984, 1985, 1988, 2006, 2010

DIVISION CHAMPIONSHIPS *(since 1970 AFL-NFL merger)*

1984, 1985, 1986, 1987, 1988, 1990, 2001, 2005, 2006, 2010, 2018

KEY COACHES

Mike Ditka (1982–92):
   106–62, 6–6 (playoffs)
George Halas (1920–29, 1933–42,
   1946–55, 1958–67): 318–148–31,
   6–3 (playoffs)

KEY PLAYERS
(position, seasons with team)

Doug Atkins (DE, 1955–66)
Dick Butkus (LB, 1965–73)
Jay Cutler (QB, 2009–16)
Danny Fortmann (G, 1936–43)
Bill George (LB, 1952–65)
Red Grange (RB, 1925, 1929–34)
Dan Hampton (DE, 1979–90)
Sid Luckman (QB, 1939–50)
Bronko Nagurski (FB-DT,
   1930–37, 1943)
Walter Payton (RB, 1975–87)
Gale Sayers (RB, 1965–71)
Mike Singletary (LB, 1981–92)
Bulldog Turner (C-LB, 1940–52)
Brian Urlacher (LB, 2000–12)

HOME FIELDS

Soldier Field (1971–2001, 2003–)
Memorial Stadium, Champaign,
   Illinois (2002)
Dyche Stadium, Evanston, Illinois
   (1970)
Wrigley Field (1921–70)
Staley Field, Decatur, Illinois (1920)

* All statistics through 2018 season

QUOTES AND ANECDOTES

George Halas had to be careful with his money because he did not have an independent income to support the Bears early on. He almost lost the team in 1933 when he barely beat a noon deadline to buy out partner Dutch Sternaman. Halas did it all in the early years, including delivering press releases to Chicago newspapers publicizing his team.

As the Bears became more financially successful, Halas kept his wallet close to him. "George Halas throws nickels around like manhole covers," tight end Mike Ditka said in 1966. An angry Halas punished Ditka by trading him to the Eagles, one of the NFL's worst teams. But Halas did not hold the grudge long, as he hired Ditka as the Bears' head coach early in 1982.

During the daytime, the CNA Center is a distinctive building in Chicago's skyline because of its red exterior. At night, when the Bears are doing well, the lights in its offices transform into a message board encouraging the team with, "GO BEARS." Building management uses a computer program to determine which lights to leave on. The CNA Center has broadcast well wishes for all of Chicago's other teams as well.

Johnny Morris, one of the Bears' all-time top receivers, later became a TV sportscaster in Chicago. One of the reasons he went into TV was to add to his modest football income. Morris said his peak Bears salary was $25,000 as a 10-year veteran in the mid-1960s. This was after he had caught an NFL-record 93 passes in 1964. So Morris would practice or play during the day, and then go to WBBM-TV to work in the evening.

Walter Payton was known for his versatility. That extended to helping the Bears' office staff. When the regular Halas Hall receptionist went to lunch, Payton sometimes took over and answered the phones. His teammates had to have eyes in the back of their heads because "Sweetness" also was the biggest prankster on the team.

GLOSSARY

archrival
An opponent that brings out great emotion in a team and its players.

berth
A place, spot, or position, such as in the NFL playoffs.

blackout
The prohibition of televising a game in the city in which it is being played if a team does not sell out its home game.

draft
The process by which teams select players who are new to the league.

franchise
An entire sports organization, including the players, coaches, and staff.

free agent
A player free to sign with any team of his choosing after his contract expires.

general manager
The executive who is in charge of the team's overall operation. He or she hires and fires coaches, drafts college players, and signs free agents.

hall of fame
A place built to honor noteworthy achievements by athletes in their respective sports.

mediocre
Neither good nor bad.

postseason
A set of games played after the regular season that decides which team will be the champion.

rookie
A first-year player.

rout
An overwhelming defeat.

showdown
A long-anticipated battle between two good or great players or teams.

MORE
INFORMATION

BOOKS

Graves, Will. *NFL's Top 10 Teams*. Minneapolis, MN: Abdo Publishing, 2017.

Myers, Jess. *NFL's Top 10 Coaches*. Minneapolis, MN: Abdo Publishing, 2018.

Ybarra, Andres. *Chicago Bears*. Minneapolis, MN: Abdo Publishing, 2017.

ONLINE RESOURCES

To learn more about the Chicago Bears, visit **abdobooklinks.com** or scan this QR code. These links are routinely monitored and updated to provide the most current information available.

PLACE TO VISIT

Bears Training Camp
Olivet Nazarene University
One University Avenue
Bourbonnais, IL 60914
800–648–1463
chicagobears.com/fan-zone/training-camp

The Bears began holding their training camp on Olivet's campus in 2002. Many of the training camp practices are open to the public in late July and early August.

INDEX

Atkins, Doug, 28

Blanda, George, 24

Briggs, Lance, 34, 36, 38, 39

Brown, Mike, 34

Butkus, Dick, 28–30, 31, 38

Casares, Rick, 26

Covert, Jimbo, 8

Cutler, Jay, 35, 36, 39–40

Dent, Richard, 8

Ditka, Mike, 8–9, 11, 28, 32

Dooley, Jim, 26, 30

Driscoll, Paddy, 26

Duerson, Dave, 8

Farrington, Bo, 28

Finks, Jim, 6, 8, 31

Forte, Matt, 38

Galimore, Willie, 28

Gault, Willie, 8

George, Bill, 26–27, 38

Glennon, Mike, 41

Grange, Red, 15–16

Grossman, Rex, 34–35

Halas, George, 8, 12–16, 18, 22, 24, 26–31

Halas, George Jr., 31

Hampton, Dan, 8

Hanie, Caleb, 38

Hay, Ralph, 14

Hester, Devin, 35

Hill, Harlon, 26

Jones, Thomas, 35

Luckman, Sid, 17, 18–23, 24, 35

Lujack, Johnny, 24

Mack, Khalil, 41

Macon, Eddie, 26

McAfee, George, 20, 23

McMahon, Jim, 7, 8–10, 35

Morris, Johnny, 28

Nagurski, Bronko, 16, 22

Orton, Kyle, 35

Pace, Ryan, 40–41

Payton, Walter, 4–7, 10–11, 31, 32, 34

Peppers, Julius, 36

Perry, William, 9–10

Piccolo, Brian, 29

Plank, Doug, 9

Robinson, Allen, 41

Ryan, Buddy, 8, 9

Sayers, Gale, 29–30, 31

Singletary, Mike, 8, 10, 38

Smith, Lovie, 34

Smith, Roquan, 38

Sprinkle, Ed, 26

Staley, A. E., 12–14

Sternaman, Dutch, 14–17

Thrower, Willie, 26

Tillman, Peanut, 34

Trubisky, Mitch, 40–41

Turner, Bulldog, 20, 23

Urlacher, Brian, 34, 36, 38, 39

ABOUT THE AUTHOR

Robert Cooper is a retired law enforcement officer and lifelong NFL fan. He and his wife live in Seattle near their only son and two grandchildren.

Dodgeville Public Library
WITHDRAWN
Dodgeville, WI 53533